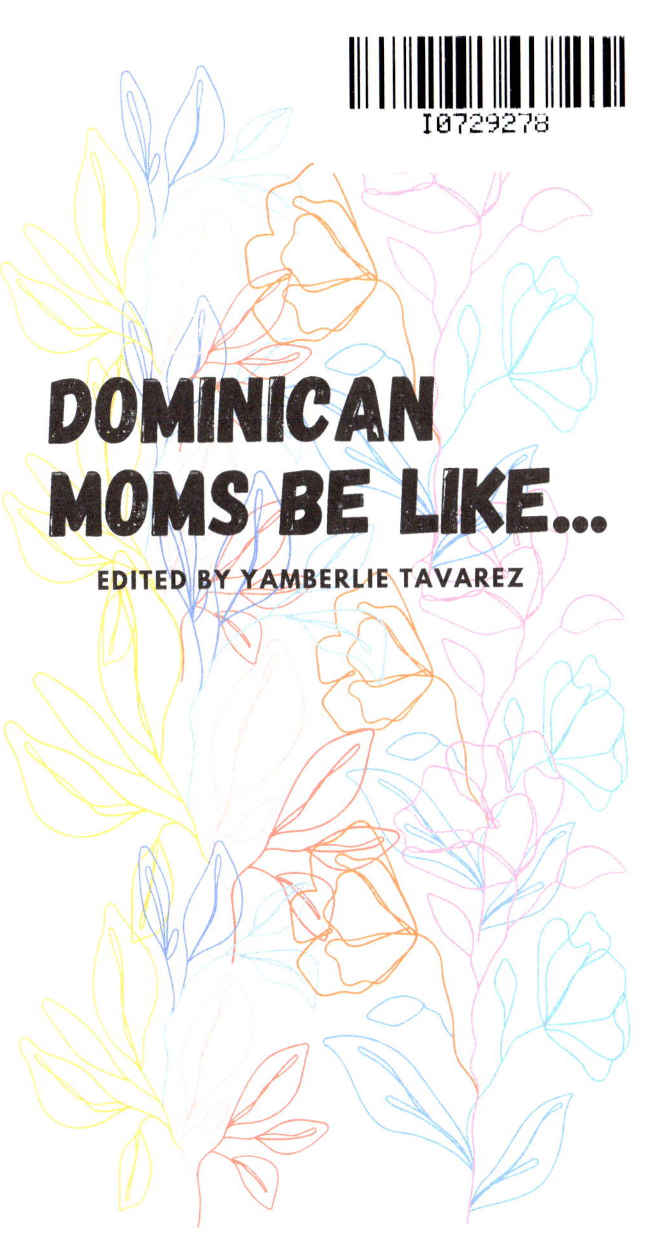

DOMINICAN MOMS BE LIKE...

EDITED BY YAMBERLIE TAVAREZ

DWA Press is an Imprint of Dominican Writers Assoc., a 501 (c)(3) non-profit literary arts organization founded in 2015 with the mission to support Dominican writers by providing them the tools and resources to become published authors.

Editor: Yamberlie Tavarez
Cover Art Design: Angela Abreu
ISBN-978-1-7372467-8-7

Published in the United States.

DWA Press
An imprint of Dominican Writers Assoc.
www.dominicanwriters.com
info@dominicanwriters.com

Las palabras de mami tienen una forma de asegurar
mi destino, "Que Dios te acompañe,"
antes de salir de casa. Me enseñaron
como confiar a la distancia,

"En la confianza esta el peligro." Y
como elegir sabiamente mis palabras,
"La lengua es el castigo del cuerpo."

Pero lo que mami no sabe,
en los dias en que apenas puedo
salir de la cama, busco sus palarabras para
sobrevivir. Como una cuerda invisible
jalandome hacia adelante, diciendome,

"Dios aprieta, pero no ahorca."

-Koylan Massiel Gomez

CONTENTS

Reflection

Amaris Castillo

Hypocrisy lodged somewhere between our mothers' lungs and arms.

We recognized it early on.

As niñas, we are told by our Dominican moms, "No le' preste' atención a lo que diga la gente. Those people don't know you. We're your best friends, the ones who count. Not these amiguitas. We're your mothers."

It takes time for young minds to emerge from this fog, this string of stern reminders. But us niñas eventually picked up on the shifts, the irony lapping at our feet like waves crashing.

Before any guests came over, nuestras madres sprang into action. They'd sweep every crevice of their apartments and plunge their worn mops into buckets of scalding water to coat the linoleum floors until all rooms smelled of lavender Mistolín.

They'd wipe the dining table even if it would later be covered in cloth; not the cheap vinyl of everyday use, but the

fancy tablecloths with the cut-out embroidered edges.

They would clean so that their fingers turned into soaked raisins and then yell at us to pick up a rag, to contribute. Then they earned accidental burns to their hand while cooking furiously.

It became apparent that our Dominican moms did indeed care about what others thought of them. We knew this by how they moved, how they arranged pillows on the couch just so, and how they tinkered with their ceramic elephants and angels—delicate like their self-image.

Their reputations and pride hinged on how well they took care of the spaces they called home. "What would our guests say if they walked into a dirty house?" our madres would say.

Everything must be immaculate. Orderly. Clean. Just as our Dominican mothers had been taught in their native homeland by their Dominican mothers, who were taught by their mothers.

As niñas, nuestras madres, and their own madres, were told that a respectable and honorable woman always keeps her house in order in case of an unannounced visita—of which there have been many.

Stay consistent, and you'd never have to worry about your ears ringing someday.

We scoffed at our mothers and eventually grew into young women, unaware that this yearning for appearances had settled deep, deep, deep inside our core. We told ourselves we were different.

But in the hours before a visitor's arrival, we, former niñas clean our homes feverishly. Maniacally.

We sweep, mop, and scrub till our lower backs pulsate and ache. We worry about dust particles that may or may not have been left undetected on the kitchen table or bathroom sink and how they'd be perceived.

Would we be thought of as indecent?

Una mujer who can't take care of her home, much less herself?

So, we continue.

And we spray Windex on our mirrors and wipe, wipe, wipe until the reflection shows just who we are.

A Comer Se Ha Dicho

Phrases Dominican mothers feed their DominicanYork children

Angelina Altagracia Vargas

Me: "Maaaaaaa, tengo hambre!"
Mami: "Ah, pues bebe agua."

Uff, besides my grandfather responding, "Ah, pues duermete y así no tienes hambre," that was the worst response my mother could've given me when I was hungry.

Growing up, I was always gordita and hungry, or so I thought. I probably confused boredom with hunger most of the time. Even so, my mother's response was always clever, which made me speculate: Dominicans don't believe in snacks.

Think about it, usually for desayuno it's—tres golpe, una avenita, or guineitos con bacalao guisao. Lunch was ready by noon, otro heavy meal—la bandera Dominicana or una berenjena guisa con salami, habichuelas y arroz blanco, yummm. Dinner could be frituras or un sandwich de eso, de salami y cheddar cheese.

But in between that? No snacks. Dominicans don't believe in snacks.

Yes, there were the patelitos, salami and cheese, and crackers with mayo/butter and cheese. Still, those hors d'oeuvres were usually reserved for special occasions like birthdays, hora santas, or noche buena.

Dominican moms be like "vengan niños!" every time food is ready. It's a tradition my mom and aunts got from their father when he raised 7 chamaquitos in La Capital with his wife.

When Dominicans arrive in the U.S., they question eurocentric eating habits. My mom and aunts would tease us and ask, "Que merienda ni merienda, espera la comida o la cena." Whenever I came across my friend's moms or other Dominicans, I found it fascinating how they had a similar habit.

As I'm writing this narrative about my family's relationship with Dominican food, I think about our gastronomy's impact on the conceptualization of race, specifically Black consciousness. Whenever I say "tengo hambre!" it's always "Ah, pues bebe agua" and never "here's a step-by-step analysis on how the conquistadors gentrified our food and used it to the island's inhumanity and demise." In society, we barely talk about food poverty, including food inflation and lack of food quality in Black and Brown neighborhoods.

I've always been in awe of how food has been a unifying factor in our culture and how giving we are through food. Whenever we go on a gira, best believe we have calderos full of food to sustain us anywhere we're at—Los 7 Lagos, Six flags, or Coney Island. When we host fiestas de palos or un maní, we have chivo con un moro negro and ensalada de papa on deck for us and for the santos. It's a culture of giving, of "everybody eats, b," in the best Ace from *Paid in Full* fashion.

Speaking of nobody pasando hambre, we were broke when we first moved from Washington Heights to The Bronx in '98. The only furniture we had were those foldable twin-sized beds, and we were in that confusing transitioning stage where my mom and aunts were applying for food stamps—a steep risk they took as they were undocumented.

Pues, one day we were hungry, like mad hungry. All we had was $12 in coins (mainly in pennies), and we walked to the supermarket to buy a bag of rice, oil, and eggs. That day, my mother and aunts managed to feed 3 adults and 4 toddlers con arroz blanco y huevo.

Ironically, my aunt told me that story on a Saturday while preparing the same meal. I told her how much I abhorred arroz con huevo growing up because of its "plainness." She reasoned that the meal was a Dominican hack making it possible to feed en masse.

Nowadays, that's my go-to meal when money is tight. I even garnish it with some parsley to remind me of the significance of food on the Ayití island.

Food has always been a communal element in my family, in every season of our lives. In Nueva Yol, these seasons are rough too. That "vengan niños!" was the best thing we could hear because it meant that, yes, we will be eating today despite the poverty and how "mala la cosas estan."

That "vengan niños" would hit so hard those sleepover nights! It was a melody to my cousins' and my ears. My mom and aunts would feed us domplines con hot dogs or salami, espaguetis con pan, or los tres golpe—all food "que rinden," like they would say.

They were also words we anticipated hearing outside the house because although those words originated inside our 2-bedroom apartment, they had no static settings. They would transcend physical space and travel to amusement parks, church trips, school events, and Claremont Park in The Bronx. Barbeques and block parties would always feed the whole block; again, "everybody eats, b!"

Me: "Maaaaaaa, tengo hambre!"
Mami: "Ah, pues bebe agua."

Words I miss now more than ever. They've now turned into:

Me: "Mami, tienes hambre? Voy a comprar comida."

Mami: "Si pero no te preocupes que yo pongo un arroz a hervir ahí y despues se averigua la acompaña."

Something about those words makes me sad and nostalgic because despite us, los muchachos, growing up and earning an income, the things we made out of poverty just feels wholesome. Latching on to the aspirations of better days was enough.

Better days that now don't seem as glamorous as we had imagined on those cold winter days, when we would whip out the pan Italianos con un chocolaton (hot cocoa with oatmeal) as our best resort to staying warm.

Now it's just us ordering food for delivery from our phones and growing frustrated because they messed up our orders yet another time. It's not the same, just as Willie Colón and Héctor Lavoe warned us, "todo tiene su final."

Times change, and we all grow up, but I will forever be grateful for how Dominican moms be like "barriga llena, corazon contento," I think that's the most beautiful thing.

I've ever heard my mom and aunts say. It signifies the joy food gives us. These words speak for all the times we told our mothers we were hungry and they, no matter what, whipped something out for us despite the circumstances.

Banda de Chismosas

Cindy Burgos

"Oye muchachita, tu no llamas," she says, skipping past the pleasantries to make her complaint known. It had only been 48 hours since our last call, but, for mami, the silence was deafening.

Audacious of me to skip a session with her. The decision is inexcusable, yet I continue to justify myself in anticipation of the comedic exchange. Our conversations open in a string of lighthearted insults—a love language she and I share. She sprinkles in a common plight, "Pero llamame para saber que estas viva," just before initiating the latest session of storytime detailing the adventures that make Ada's life a full one.

Doña Ada, as I lovingly refer to her, is a loud, raspy-voiced woman bursting at the seams with wit, tales, and laughter—her anecdote to life's woes. She swears that limonsillos were responsible for her lack of a whisper to this day. However, given her presence in our community, her volume is a gift of divine intervention. She wields her words to counsel and encourage her tribe through story, never one to withhold her love. It is this sacred exchange that makes every one of our conversations unique.

Proceeding with a request that needs no permission, she begins her stories with "Dejame decirte..." priming my heart for the lessons. Elaborating in detail and stroking a blank canvas in context, I find my spirit transported to her dining table. Seated before a spread of all my favorites—tostones, asopao de camarones, una limonada fresca o copita de vino. A little sip here, a little sip there, and suddenly I'm immersed in familiar ancestral tradition.

Whether the experience she divulges is profound or not, she calls it "una bobería." Yet, diligently, I cling to her every word. Allowing them to send waves through my core. With laughter, I am home. With every nugget of wisdom, I am grounded. I see more of her revealed with every story shared —gratitude, regrets, joy, and longing. At the end of it all, my love abounds, and so does my desire for healing.

"Ya te dejo. Tu eres muy chismosa", she says. To which I quip, "Y tu la reina de los chismosos." "Gracias mi hija," she responds, offended but accepting.

Our exchange is sealed and passed on for the next generation to relish. Turning experiences that would have otherwise crushed her spirit into nostalgic bites of relayed and reframed celebration. Her stories are an invitation to a practice in gratitude. A call to embrace the challenges instead of bracing. It is among the sweetest gifts she's

imparted over me. And while chismosa is far from an inherited quality, she leverages the insult to keep me in suspense until our next session.

¡Como los Chivos Sin Ley!

Henry Suarez

Mira, ahi estaba llamando una tal Karina. ¿Quien es esa muchachita?

Una niña de mi clase, Mami.

Bueno mas te vale que te ponga para tus estudios y deje tranquilla a esas niñas.

Coming home from playing football, this is how mami greeted me at the door. As the mother of three boys, she was always suspicious anytime a girl would call the house. In this case, Karina was calling about a group project. Still, it immediately put mami on high alert. She would threaten us with a pela if we got a girl pregnant. Our hypothetical girlfriend would also get a pela. She assumed the task of punishing both of us in this theoretical teen pregnancy.

The first time I brought a girl home, she and my dad were friendly enough. They had her over for dinner and enjoyed some small talk. They then read me a sermon about not allowing this relationship to affect my grades when she left. Grades that were not good anyway, but I guess they wanted

to make any point. Mami followed it up with a one-liner the next day before leaving for work, "Mira, mucho cuidado lo que tu anda haciendo con esa noviecita."

She's very protective of her boys. She takes personal offense if we say something negative about ourselves, as though it reflects poorly on what she's done as a parent. Worst of all is when my brothers and I fight or if we aren't speaking for any reason. You see it in her eyes, the pain of her babies being offended by another one of her babies! All she says is "Mis hijos, los hermanos hay que cuidarlos."

One thing that can't be denied is that she can throw down in the kitchen. Growing up, our house was the go-to place. We always seemed to have some hungry ass friends, more than happy to come over for a bowl of whatever mami was cooking. My dad would always complain about the noise level, especially when trying to take an after-work nap. To mami, though, having a house full of kids always seemed to bring her joy.

Even if we came over with more kids than there was food, she would quickly whip up some more food or pull out the leftovers. Mami is the type that cooks extra just because, so there's always leftover food. "Pa que falte, que sobre!" The thought of letting a kid go hungry was upsetting to her. It's a must that everyone leaves the house with their stomach on

the verge of exploding. The plates that she puts out for people are ridiculous. It's a mountain of rice and like half a pot of beans.

This seemed like the best of both worlds because it allowed us to hang out, and she could rest easy knowing we were safe. She's a worrier by nature; she constantly worries about where we are and whom we are with. She never liked the idea of us spending much time in other people's homes. "Uno nunca sabe de lo que otra gente son capaz." By that logic, wouldn't other parents wonder what went on in our house?

Hanging out in front of our building, the night would constantly be interrupted by the creaking sound of our bedroom window, followed by "Henry, Ariel ya suban." One night she popped her head out the window, exclaiming:

¡Mis hijos ya son la 1:30, suban que es un dia de semana!

We were already teenagers at the time, and it was during summer break. Either way, that time didn't seem accurate.

I replied, "Mami, mueva el reloj y mire la hora de nuevo."

¡Bueno, las 11:30 no son hora de estar en la calle, suban!

There was no arguing at that point; we had to head upstairs.

Arriving at home, late at night and usually drunk, we could see her as we came through the door. Standing in the kitchen doorway in her bata, she'd start her interrogation. Asked if we were drunk. Telling us to go wash off the smell of romo.

She's the type that won't fall asleep until the last one of us arrives. I'd be out partying and get a text from her saying, "Mi hijo, ya ven a tu casa." A grown man getting texts from his mom about when I'm coming home... serves me right for living there until my mid 20's.

Like any typical kid, I would find some of her ways to be overbearing. Now that I'm a parent, I have a greater appreciation for what she was going through. You want to ensure that your family is safe; there is no greater duty.

Much of what goes into my mother's parenting method comes from the void she felt as a child. The attention and the care she provided us were what she longed for. Had she gone out at night, there likely wouldn't be anyone worrying about her whereabouts. Meanwhile, she was unable to sleep until we made it home safely.

As is often the case in DR, mami wasn't raised by her parents. "Mira muchacho, yo andaba de casa en casa, como una ectera." At 12, she arrived at the home of my grandmother's sister. This aunt and her husband helped

retrieve her birth certificate and enroll her in school. As she recalls, "Ahi fue que yo por fin vi la gloria."

Mami, a reference book for refranes, got one for almost every occasion. She discourages late-night snacking: "Come lo que vas a comer ahora, y cierra con broches de oro." Whenever we look messy, "Tu parece una gallina mata a escobazo." If we did things without permission, we'd hear, "Ustedes andan por ahi como chivos sin ley." If she finds something to be overhyped or lackluster, she says, "Es mas la sal, que el chivo." She loves to say, "Me hice la chiva loca" to describe when she has played dumb or feigned ignorance. Goats seem to make for great use in phrases.

I have battled weight issues my entire life, and mami is the first to say, "Hijo tu tienes que rebajar un poco." I'll mention that I'll be skipping dinner to do some intermittent fasting. She's then worried, "Pero no es pasar hambre tampoco." Anytime I go on a diet and lose substantial weight, she wonders if I haven't done some irreparable damage and won't be able to stop losing weight.

Mami is also the type to check in daily. We speak almost every day by phone. Even if it's just to see how my commute was to work. Of course, for me, it's easier to send a text, but she responds to texts with a call. She calls nightly to see about her granddaughters; the only problem is she calls

when we're putting them down.

¿Y las mujeres, ya se durmieron?

¡Mami! Estamos en eso, la llamo ahorita.

Si, si esta bien mi hijo.

At this point, shame on me for even picking up. In my defense, though, she and my dad are at an age where I see the call, and immediately I'm worried. I also can't send a message saying, "La llamo en un ratito" because she'll just call again.

My greatest vulnerability is my children and what could happen to them outside my care. Finding good childcare is an enormous challenge; trusting them is no easy task, and reasonable pricing is unheard of. When our daughters started school, my parents volunteered to help with drop-off/pick-up. My wife and I greatly appreciate the assistance. The fact that my parents do it for free is a blessing. The folded laundry is the cherry on top.

Alas, some things come along with family that one wouldn't get from hiring a stranger. Having my middle daughter point out that "Abuela dijo que esas galletitas son para las niñas y no para ti," for example, or when I go for a second serving of

food and my oldest daughter exclaims, "Dice abuela que tu no tienes necesidad de servirte mas de una vez," seems like a bit much. It's absolutely unnecessary; she's trained my children to shame me in my own home.

While I could do without the judgment, it truly is great to have her around the girls. She always tells me of their adventures walking to and from the bus stop. Meanwhile, the girls always fill me in on their afterschool meals.

“Papi, abuela hizo pure de papa, pero el tuyo es mejor.” Abuela doesn’t know her recipes have undergone some changes.

I benefitted from having parents who were present and caring; that nurtured me into the man I am today. My mother wasn't as fortunate; she suffered through many difficult moments but overcame unimaginable odds. Her nature as a protector has been to guide her children and ensure they had what she never did.

For this, I am eternally grateful. Words will always fall short, but they're a start.

¡Gracias mami!

Eso te Pasa Por Ser Freca

Luz Mack

I don't know how my grandmother was as a child, but I knew mamá Luz as kind, quiet, giving, stoic; a devout catholic who many hoped to emulate. In all her wisdom, my mother named me after my saintly grandmother, someone I was nothing like.

With time, I was given the nickname Luchy. I'm not entirely certain how I transitioned from Luz Maria to Luchy. Still, of one thing I was sure, it was bestowed upon me because of my ever curious, can't sit still, and a lot to handle ways.

I've been told stories of all the messes I got into. Like how I never learned to walk, I just took off running one day. My mom said it was a sign from God letting her know I would never slow down! I can still hear my mother calling me zángana because I would run around barefoot, getting everything dirty with my blacktop feet. I loved feeling the soft ground.

I wanted to look like my mom on one occasion, so I grabbed her mascara and smeared it all over my forehead.

My beautiful mother grabbed me and gently cleaned all the smeared black mascara smudges off my face. If that had happened now, I'm sure that moment would have been instagrammable, but at the time, I received many unpleasant looks.

One day, I ran up to my mother to get her attention and show her a small baby chick captured and placed behind my back. Releasing the baby chick's beak, I opened my mouth to fool people into thinking it was me singing like a pio-pio (as I called it). My aunt swayed on her rocking chair, looking the other way, begging me to let the poor baby chick be.

Yeah, I was a curious one growing up. In a place where curiosity was frowned upon and often referred to as 'jodiendo, I never heard any Dominican child be encouraged to explore. We were expected to sit still, help at home, and follow the example of our elders.

My mother found some of my troublesome acts humorous. Still, when it was time to take me to church, she would remind me that she was raising a good Christian girl, and let's face it, nowhere in the bible do you hear "good" people behaving the way I did. Though there must have been a Dominican bible because older folks would unanimously exclaim, "Ta bueno' por freca" or “no sea frekita!"

I don't remember the first time hearing such expression, but it was clear to me how it wasn't good to be freca. It would be met with pain and discomfort when incidents took place, and I knew it was karma for not staying still. I was often reminded that wrongdoings were paid for instantly. I remember wailing in pain when I got hurt and being told, "Eso te pasa por ser freca."

My younger sisters were tasked to help me behave like them because they were well mannered, pleasant, and poised; what adults would refer to as easy to watch.

When we left our beloved Santiago to live in a tiny two-bedroom apartment in Washington Heights, we held tightly to each other and our identity. It was hard for my mother to learn and adapt and push our small family forward. She enrolled me in school, cared for my younger sister at home, whilst helping my father work in a bodega. We were the first minority family in a Caucasian community, and we stood out! For the most part, we had kind neighbors, but we also knew which ones to stay away from.

Despite how much of a troublemaker I was as a child, I was covered by my mother's love. She was there holding me when someone looked at me, curious about why I was darker than my siblings, or thought it was okay to call me “the black one.” When I was distraught that I didn't look like her with fair skin and green eyes.

When she saw me crying because my eyes were not as blue as, or my dark hair tied up in three buns didn't look like, my blonde white doll. She would tell me that I resembled her and my grandma the most out of her children.

There are so many moments that her love overshadowed all my freca ways. She did everything to raise me right and always stood by me. It's what I strive to pass on to my family.

As I watch my mother doting on her grandchildren, I can't help but feel slightly envious. She bounces my babies on her lap, singing beautiful nothings, delighting in the butterfly kisses on their cheeks. I adore how she continues to shower them with endless affection, lovingly becoming their Tita' as they've grown older. Tita is committed to ensuring that they spend time with her no matter how busy life gets. They know she will comfort them with good food, prayer, snuggles, and conversation until they are better. Their relationship, an unshakeable bond, continues to flourish.

My kids won't contain their rambunctious energy after a grueling school day. They climb over the sofa and chairs until they are laughing uncontrollably, or until someone gets hurt. If Tita is around, they rush, wailing to her as she cuddles them. She'll lovingly say, "Ven pa' recogerte," ensuring them all is well.

This is the same lady who would remind my siblings and me, "Eso le pasa por freca!" when we were jodiendo la pita and would get hurt. My kids would never know how these words became life's idiom and a point of self-reflection. I'm happy this particular phrase won't plague my kids because all they know is Tita's boundless affection.

Recently I found myself at home healing from leg surgery. Everything felt amiss, and I couldn't help but sense that perhaps I did something to deserve this. I called my mother, but it was hard for me to tell her I was hurting. She arrived offering to clean the house and cook a meal, yet all I yearned for was for her presence by my side. She didn't have to tell me, "Ven pa recogerte." It was enough to feel her close.

As we rested there on my couch doing nothing with my leg elevated on three pillows and my crutches nearby, she imparted on me how unfortunate events in our lives are unavoidable, as there is always a lesson or a blessing before you. My resilience, she professed, had led me here to this place in my life, and she couldn't wait to see how far it would get me!

It was the first time I felt I was no longer freca, that maybe not everything was happening to me, and that my curiosity had in truth led me to self-discovery.

She still always knows what I need.

The Mamiti

Mauricio Castillo

My mother is a stereotype killer.

I'm sure you've heard of the stereotype surrounding Dominican mothers and their sons. Countless stories exchanged, complaints made (usually by fathers, sisters, and girlfriends), and memes meme'd.

You've seen them. The mom yells at the waiter and carries her 40-year-old son like an infant when his order is incorrect. The mom faints because her son's girlfriend didn't fix him a plate.

The Dominican mother-son relationship is a defining characteristic of our culture. The mother sees the son not as just a son but as a king who can do no wrong. This lasts a lifetime; no matter how old or young or how good or bad he is, the son will forever be a sparkle in his mother's eye.

Shit, seeing how Cersei was with Joffrey in Game of Thrones made me wonder if she was from El Cibao instead of Casterly Rock.

The American variant of this stereotype is called "Momma's Boy."

I call it, "The Mamiti."

The mamiti is real. The mamiti is strong. The mamiti is something I never experienced with my mother. And I didn't realize how rare that actually was in Dominican culture until I was much, much older.

My mother—Maria Amparo Del Carmen (affectionally known as la Cacharra)—had me at 31 years old, five years after my older sister and seven years after she immigrated to this country. She made 5'2" look tall, runway model-skinny with a big black poof of wavy hair and large, owl-like eyes—at least, that's how she looked in old pictures. I, of course, never saw her that way in person, and she never ceased to remind me that it was my fault she wasn't built like a teenager anymore. I apparently tore through her body during birth like the Kool-Aid Man, if you hear her tell it. "Tu acabaste con el cuerpo que yo tenia," she would say.

OK, I know that sounds horrible, but I have to admit I'm laughing as I write this. You see, la Cacharra is nothing if not a dry comedian, and one of her favorite jokes is how I (not my sister, who came first) ruined her thim-slick body. That dry, potentially trauma-inducing humor (hey, I'm nothing if not self-aware) is just one of the many ways she continues to be a splash of color in a sea of grey, exhausted Dominican mothers who look at their sons like the sun shines out their asses.

And as my mother, she was well aware of what actually came out of my butt, and it definitely wasn't the sun—and she let me know it, too.

I remember being a chubby eight-year-old—chubby in that if we were cursed with the mamiti, she'd be like, "Mi hijo esta fuerte!" and I'd flex, and she'd laugh and kiss me kind of way. There would be food and lots of it. As a chubby eight-year-old, I wanted a lot of it. And I out-ate all my scrawny cousins in speed, efficiency, and total output (input?). So, when I inhaled my plate of rice (half of which was concon), beans, and pollo guisado, I looked around expectantly, hoping a sympathetic aunt or older cousin would see me and say those magic words: "Mauri, tu quiere mas?"

Instead, my grandmother noticed, and she, fueled with the strength of the mamiti, instantly shot forward as if from a cannon, grabbed my plate, and said, "Te voy a buscar mas."

My mother saw this, stood up and proclaimed, "No! Ese muchacho esta DEMASIADO GORDO!"

My cousins burst out laughing, and seething anger replaced any want for more food I had. She humiliated me in front of everyone, laughing while she did it.

Of course, my grandmother was undeterred, and so was the mamiti. She seemed to swell with the rage that comes from seeing a "son" done wrong. She called my mother crazy, said I was a growing boy, and that she should know better. She filled me with a plate that might've been bigger than my first one.

That was the end of it; my mother could do nothing to stop her mother.

I grinned widely as Grandma brought me the plate, but I saw the mask of disappointment on my mother's face. Whether for being a glutton or relishing in her mother's mamiti completely smothering her powers as the anti-mamiti avatar, I don't know.

I just know I've never forgotten that day because it's one of my earliest memories of realizing that my mother wasn't like other mothers. Yet, from that day forward, I started being more equitable with my meals, and the baby weight that was the subject of jokes from cousins and classmates soon disappeared.

I was around the same age when my mother played the shit out of me in my own house.

Like many Dominican mothers, she did most, if not all, the chores. My sister was already getting into that "I'm too cool to listen to my parents" stage, so she wasn't any help. My father was the breadwinner, and while he knew how to cook and clean, I don't remember him grabbing so much as a rag when I was young. Even when my mother held part-time jobs to make ends meet, she still did all the housework.

Until, of course, she caught me in her trap. She had been cleaning the bathroom one Saturday; her forearms pumped from all the scrubbing. I don't remember if I happened to walk by or if I went to use the sink, but she took one look at me and said, "Tu dique no priva en fuerte? Ve aver quien estrega mas."

Being a dumb kid, I didn't know her plot. I just saw an opportunity to show off my "muscles." Before long, I was scrubbing THEEEEE SHIT out of that tub.

I found her laid up on the couch watching Univision when I finished.

The precedent had been set, though. From that day forward, I did dishes, did laundry, and cleaned. When I told my male Dominican compatriots in casual conversation, they looked at me in horror. I was some perverted version of Cinderella, and my mother was an evil witch.

I never noticed. I never thought she was taking advantage of me or being mean to me. I thought it was normal. It wasn't until later in life that I learned of the mamiti, but it was too late by then. She had done her job well.

I grew up with her being distant and frigid, treating me more like a young friend she had to take care of instead of the golden child that Dominican mothers usually saw their sons as. She "Mira, tu'd" me almost as much as she used my name.

But there were signs of softness in her, too. Chinks in the anti-mamiti armor. She confided in me. She joked with me the way two homies might tease each other. She didn't encourage my non-traditional hobbies of drawing, reading, and writing. Still, she didn't shut them down either, not like others did. She was protective, maybe to a fault.

My sister and I grew up in a rough project that was relatively devoid of children our age, so playing outside without supervision was a no-go. God forbid we tried to go out when the sun went down; you would think she was trying to shield us from vampires. "Tu ta loco!" she would exclaim at my simple request to play baseball outside. My mother never even liked us to be babysat when she wasn't around.

But while my sister found it annoying (her rebelliousness against my mother's iron fist ripped a chasm between them that has never really gone away), my cousins made fun of me because she was so strict and harsh and never let me sleepover or "do hood shit with my friends," I didn't care.

I might've gotten mad at the moment the way a kid might get upset with their parent for not letting them do something, but it was never a big deal to me. I almost preferred she be mean than overly affectionate; I welcomed the consequences instead of growing up thinking I could do no wrong (of course, that could be years of brainwashing talking, but still). Shit, I took one listen to "Amor de Madre" by Aventura and said to myself, "Thank God mami wasn't like that with me."

And I had seen the results of the mamiti firsthand in friends and family—sons who were either unprepared for life or who treated their mothers like servants.

Because that's the gist of it, isn't it? My mother was nails, treating me more like a boxing trainer might treat a less-than-talented prospect than a doting mom to a beloved son, but not because she didn't like me or love me. But because she knew the world was a cold, dirty place, the best way to prepare me for that was to give me a taste of it at home.

Or maybe it was because she had been overly affectionate with my sister, only for my sister to ignore and take her for granted. Perhaps, at that point, la Cacharra said, "I will not make the same mistake twice—not with him."

Or maybe something happened in her youth that made her realize the more beneficial style of parenting is to keep your kids at arm's reach so that they don't get too clingy and not to shower them with love because when the world fucks them up, they'll be able to get back up, wipe the blood off their mouths and smile.

These are all thoughts I've had, looking back on my youth. I don't know the true answer. My mother practices plausible deniability whenever I try to ask, "Hey, why were you/are you so mean to me?" Remember the Chappelle's Show skit, "I plead da FIF"? That's her, except she says, "Yo? Que yo era mala contigo? Yo no me acuerdo de eso," with the same faux-innocence a serial killer talking to a detective might have.

I just know that when I struggled to find a job as a writer, depressed and hopeless, she was there in my iron will to keep moving forward. When I moved out and got my first place, she was there in all the navigational skills I had developed for the trials that come with being an independent adult.

Even something as simple, yet as necessary, as cleaning my fucking bathroom now—she's there.

I don't remember my mother ever kissing my face. Even after I moved out, I don't remember her giving me a non-New-Year's-Eve-at-midnight, full-on hug. I heard, "Tu va ver" more than something like "Mi hijo lindo." She'll ask, "Y tu no le has buscado un plato a Natasha [my girlfriend]?"—not the other way around. All the hallmarks of the mamiti that I know of now; she did the opposite.

But I wouldn't trade la Cacharra—I wouldn't trade the years of hilarious, borderline-bully-like, cold-but-made-you-feel-like-you-were-her-equal mothering—for anything. Because I love who I am today, and I wouldn't be that person without her and how she raised me.

My mother broke the cycle. And I wouldn't trade any of it —not even for a lifetime of the mamiti.

Contributing Writers

Amaris Castillo is a journalist and the creator of Bodega Stories—a series featuring real stories from the corner store. Born in Brooklyn, New York, to Dominican parents, she credits the many tales she heard growing up to her love of storytelling. Amaris' writing has appeared in The New York Times, Remezcla, Latina Magazine, and Parents Latina Magazine. You can catch her writing from her home office, just a few steps away from her windowsill lined with her muñecas sin rostro.

Angelina Altagracia Vargas is an Afro Dominican storyteller, educator, and agent of change from The Bronx. She graduated with a Bachelor of Science in Critical Foundations of Education and a Bachelor of Arts in Women and Gender Studies from Syracuse University. Angelina received a Master of Science in Education in Bilingual Childhood Education from The City College of New York. She is pursuing her Ph.D. in Urban Education at The University of Maryland. When she's not reading or making cooking videos, you can find her traveling around the world or studying at a nearby café.

Cindy Burgos is a first-generation Dominican-American storyteller and writer. She is the creator of a blog called spltends that reflects on and unpacks bicultural experience through the lens of identity, generational trauma, healing, motherhood, and more. Originally from NYC's "Little Dominican Republic," Washington Heights, she resides in Atlanta, Georgia, with her husband and daughter.

Henry Suarez is a Dominican-American writer, born and raised in Corona, Queens. He now resides in Westchester, NY, with his wife and daughters. His writing focuses mainly on the immigrant experience, growing up bicultural/bilingual, and his journey through fatherhood.

Luz Maria Mack was born in Villa Mella, Dominican Republic, and immigrated to the United States as a young child with her family. She comes from a big, loving family that is a recipe for laughter and many beautiful memories. Luz earned a Master's degree in Public Administration from Metropolitan College of New York and worked as a healthcare professional in New York City.

Mauricio (Mo) Castillo was born and raised in Queens, New York City, a first-generation Dominican-American by way of Bonao, Dominican Republic. His first love is and always will be fiction and creative writing; he was published at 18 and never looked back. He enjoys music, film, food, fitness, beer, and sound, deep conversation when he's not trying and failing to write the next great vampire novel. He is the current Senior Editor of fantasy sports content at Yahoo Sports.

www.ingramcontent.com/pod-product-compliance
Lightning Source LLC
Chambersburg PA
CBHW061225210726
48294CB00006B/1980
9781737246787